African Canadians • Achievem

IN
OUR
Time

Illustrated by Henry V. Bishop

Written by Robert Ffrench

Black Star
Books

Black Star Books
P.O. Box 28058
Dartmouth, Nova Scotia, Canada
B2W 6E2
Phone (902) 542-1388

This publication was made possible through the
financial contribution of the Nova Scotia Department
of Supply and Services.

Editor	Susan Lucy
Graphic Design	Chris Cairns. Designed as a companion piece to *Out of the Past and Into the Future*.
Filmmaker	Nova Scotia Digital Technologies Inc.
Printed by	McCurdy Printing and Typesetting Ltd.

The tape that accompanies this book was recorded with the
financial assistance of the Canada–Nova Scotia Cooperation
Agreement on Cultural Development. The songs were performed by the Nova Scotia Mass Choir under the direction of
Mr. Woody Woods. The choir's recording of "Siyahumb'e" is
included courtesy of CBC Radio, Halifax.

For additional copies of the tape, send $9.95 plus $3.00
postage and handling and 7% GST to Black Star Books at the
address above.

Canadian Cataloguing in Publication Data
    Ffrench, Robert, 1959–
        In our time
        (African Canadian achievement)
        Includes bibliographic references.
        ISBN 0–9698350–1–9

1. Blacks – Canada – History – Juvenile literature. 2. Blacks
– Canada – Biography – Juvenile literature. 3. Blacks –
Canada – History – Problems, exercises, etc. – Juvenile literature. 4. Blacks – Canada – Biography – Problems, exercises,
etc. – Juvenile literature. I. Title. II. Series: Ffrench, Robert,
1959– African Canadian achievement.

FC106.B6F46 1995   j971'.00496   C95–950030–8
F1035.N3F46 1995

Contents

Dedication

This book is dedicated to the memory of the Honourable Marcus Mosiah Garvey, who taught that self-reliance is the only true course to take in seeking equality.

The Black Star still shines!

To my children, Whitney and Ellis, I hope that their journey through life is filled with discovery and pride in themselves and their heritage.

Robert Ffrench

In pursuing the path of knowledge and sharpening my skills as a visual artist, I dedicate this book to my family. They have inspired me to keep my pride alive and share the spirit of achievement.

Peace and love.

Henry Bishop

Preface

In Canada some people identify themselves by the land or country their ancestors came from. German Canadians originally came from Germany, Scottish Canadians from Scotland.

Africans are found all over the world and while many changes have occurred since the forced movement of the slave trade, a common history starting on the continent of Africa unites all of its people. So this book will use the term African Canadian or Africans in Canada when describing the people who share this ancestry.

Introduction

Heritage and culture are a part of us all. No matter what our nationality or where our parents or grandparents came from, we all have a history.

African Canadians have a strong, proud history developed over thousands of years. A common link between the past and the present is the determination Africans have shown to be innovators and pioneers in all areas of society. Overcoming racism and jealousy, African Canadians have fought long and hard for equality. Each generation sees new leaders and role models emerge.

In Our Time highlights three important theme sections: communities, music, and achievers. In each of these themes, the past is linked with the present. Communities have provided bases where Africans in Canada have created their unique identity. Music has linked the rhythms of the continent of Africa with the people's hope for the future, while giving strength in their daily lives. And those selected for the achievers section are prominent African Canadians who have built on their own experiences and those of their people to be role models for all Canadians.

Studying and learning about the achievements of African Canadians will help develop positive self-images and understanding among people of all backgrounds. The books in this series—*Out of the Past Into the Future* and *In Our Time*—are intended to be informative and fun and to allow the reader to learn more about the contributions of African Canadians and the effect their efforts have had on all of us.

Beginnings

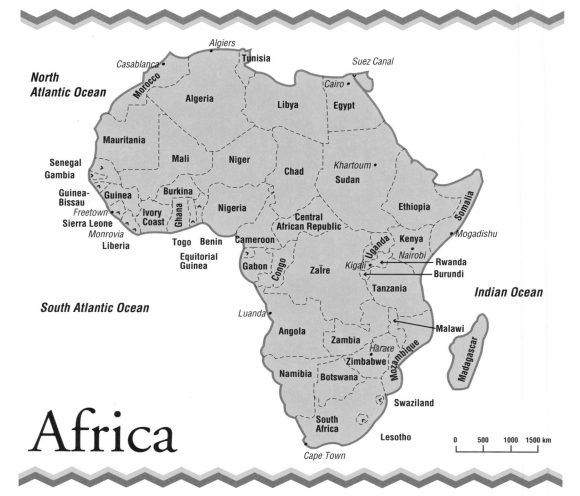

Africa

Africa is the birthplace of civilization. It is the second largest continent in the world and has over 50 countries located on it. Many of those countries have grown from historic communities that were present hundreds of years before European communities reached a civilized level. The contributions of Africans to history have been remarkable: the first known written language called hieroglyphics, the first university, the development of mathematics and science, even the first clocks and calendars.

With the start of the slave trade, much of the progress and development slowed as the best and brightest Africans were captured and made hostage. It is estimated that over 100 million people were seized by force and enslaved. However, only about 10 million arrived in the new worlds. For every 10 Africans who were captured, only one survived the voyage across the Atlantic Ocean. The rest died along the way.

The African spirit, once confined to one continent, now is found in North and South America, the Caribbean, Mexico, and other countries throughout the world.

Activity: *Be an African Penpal*

Imagine you live on the continent of Africa. Write a letter to someone in Canada explaining what life is like. Choose a country from the map of the continent as your home. It would be helpful to find out about the country before you begin. Ask a classmate, a teacher, or your parents to be your penpal. You may want to include the country's name, flag, major cities, animals found there, and other facts that will give your penpal a good understanding of your life.

Dear _____

_____

_____

_____

_____

_____

_____

_____

_____

_____

_____

_____

_____

1628   Olive le Jeune, a boy from Madagascar, is purchased in New France.

Activity: *Break the Codes*

a) Identify and break the code for each quote, to find the names of famous people of African descent.

1. If there is no struggle, there is no progress.

⊏⌃⊐⊐⌃⌃⌐⌐⊐ ⊒⊏⌐⌃⌐⌐ _____

2. No person is your friend who demands your silence, or denies you the right to grow.

⊒⌱⌐⊏⊐ ⊏⊒⌱⌱⊐⌃ _____

3. I have a dream that my four little children will one day live in a nation where they will not be judged by the colour of there skin but by the content of their character.

⊐⌱⌃⌐⊏⌱ ⌱⌐⌐⊐⌐⌃ ⊐⊏⌱⊓ _____

4. Strategy is better than strength.

⊓⌐⌐⌐⌐ ⌱⌐⊓⌱⌱⊐ _____

5. "I started with this idea in my head, "there's two things I've got a right to, death and liberty."

⊓⌐⌃⌃⌐⊏⌱ ⌱⌱⌱⌐⌱⌱ _____

6. Don't count your chickens before they are hatched.

⌱⊐⌱⌱⌐⌱ _____

7. No two people on Earth are alike and it's got to be that way in music or it isn't music.

⌱⌐⌱⌱⌐⌐⊏ ⊓⌱⌱⌐⌐⊐⌐⊓ _____

8. If you have no confidence in self, you are twice defeated in the race of life. With confidence you have won even before you have started.

⊐⌱⌃⌱⌱⌐⌱ ⊓⌱⌃⊐⊐⊓ _____

9. Education is our passport to the future, for tomorrow belongs to the people who prepare for it today.

⊐⌱⌱⌱⌱⌱⌱⌱ ⊓ _____

b) Then, choose one of the people, find out as much as you can about them, and write a short report.

The Fight Against Slavery

The African slave trade lasted for approximately 350 years. During that time millions of young Africans were stolen from their homes and sold to provide a cheap work force for the colonies of the New World. The hostages were transported in the worst conditions imaginable. The Portuguese word for the ships that carried the Africans was 'tomberos', which means coffin.

While held captive, however, many of the people promised never to give up their goal of freedom. Their determination led to over 200 slave uprisings in the United States alone during the period in which slavery was legal. The Africans did not just want personal freedom. Some like Gabriel Prosser who lived from approximately 1775 to 1800 wanted to set up an African state in the Virginia district.

As time passed other leaders emerged. Nat Turner was one who, in 1831, led the largest slave revolt in United States history.

These revolts were inspired by the efforts of Toussaint L'Ouverture who led the most famous slave uprising. This occurred in 1794 on the island of Haiti where the African hostages fought against and eventually defeated the French. Their success led to the birth of a new country governed by the former slaves. Haiti also became the first independent country in the Caribbean.

Another famous group of freedom fighters, the Maroons of Jamaica, played a part in the history of Canada. Their story is told in the first book in this series: *Out of the Past, Into the Future*.

Activity: *Illustrate a Problem*

1. Design and draw a scene or image showing the difficulties slaves endured.
   Use information you already have or that you can find out from other sources to help your efforts.

2. Design and draw a scene or image showing a problem in our world today that you wish you could change.

C o m m u n i t i e s

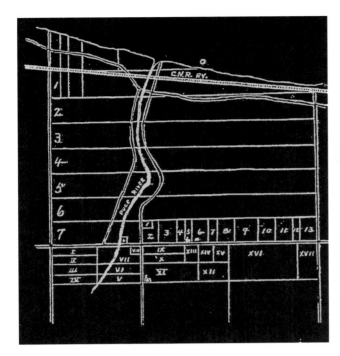

*The Refugee's
Home Society,
Detroit 1853.*

*Lot T. East Puce
River. Maidstone
Tp. Essex County*

Africans have always held strong bonds to the communities in which they live. Before their transport to North America and other parts of the world, communities were found, and continue to be found, throughout Africa. Among the proud names were Masai, Zulu, Bantu, and Nubian. These communities were highly developed societies with doctors, teachers, business people, farmers, and government.

The first group of former slaves came to Canada during the American Revolution. They became known as the Black Loyalists. As a reward for not joining the Americans who had rebelled against Great Britain, they were given land grants. However the grants were small, and the land was often the worst possible for farming. The disappointment of very poor land, difficult climate, and the level of racism amongst their white neighbours caused many to leave. Some returned to Africa and to a British colony called Sierra Leone. They hoped life there would be better. Those who remained continued their struggle for equality and freedom.

As former slaves came to Canada, it was natural that they would want to join in building communities in their new country. Many who set up these communities were prominent and well known. However, racism forced the African Canadians to the outskirts of white towns. The people were free, yet they were not free to live where they wanted.

1734   Attempting to escape slavery, Marie Joseph Angelique of Montreal sets fire to her owner's home. The fire gets out of control and spreads, causing great damage. After her capture she is put on trial and sentenced to death as an example to others.

Birchtown, Nova Scotia

The remnants of the oldest settlement of free African people in North America are found in Birchtown, Nova Scotia.

During the last days of the Revolutionary War (1775–83), a site was chosen to be a settlement for the people who stayed loyal to Great Britain. The settlers decided to call this community Shelburne.

Among the first settlers in 1783 was a group called the Black Pioneers. These were free men who had served in the army and helped to build the new town. They also set up their own community on the outskirts of Shelburne. It was called Birchtown after a former commanding officer, General Samuel Birch. By 1784 about 1,500 Africans from America were living in the community.

Like the white Loyalists the Africans were promised land for their loyalty. These land grants were intended to be equal. In reality they were very unequal. The land provided was much smaller, most often very difficult to reach, and unsuitable for farming.

The community began to disappear as the town of Shelburne continued to grow in size, and the original families moved, trying to find better areas to live. The significance of this community today is its place in history as the first community for free Africans in North America.

Amherstburg, Ontario

Amherstburg is located near Lake Erie on the Detroit River, which forms part of the boundary between Canada and the United States.

Originally founded as a loyalist settlement, it was an important early settlement site for former slaves. The Detroit River narrows at Amherstburg, so it was a good place for fugitives to cross to safety. Many made their homes there, and it became the centre for the African population in Upper Canada.

Amherstburg was visited in 1844 by Levi Coffin, who was known as the "President" of the Underground Railroad. Mr. Coffin remarked that Amherstburg was the most important terminal on the Underground Railroad.

As the community grew larger, tension grew between the white community and the new settlers. Fear and racism caused the white residents to ask that soldiers located in nearby Fort Malden not be removed from the region. They felt that without the troops they would be helpless against the large number of Africans living in the area.

Some churches discriminated against the Africans and did not allow them to take part in church services. In reaction, the African community members of Amherstburg in 1845 formed the Amherstburg Regular Missionary Association. This served to start the process of the community members' depending on each other rather than their white neighbours.

1777   The State of Vermont in the United States abolishes slavery and becomes the destination of slaves escaping from Canada.

13

Activity: *Write the text for this cartoon, using your knowledge*
of the escape to Canada by refugee slaves.

The Elgin Settlement / Buxton, Ontario

The Elgin Settlement, also known as the Buxton Mission, was the idea of Presbyterian minister William King. King was a missionary and active abolitionist. He became friends with many Africans from the United States who had moved into the district around Chatham, Ontario.

King saw a need to establish a site where the people who had once been slaves could be safe and free. He knew his vision would be possible only if the Africans owned their land. They also needed to learn to be independent by not relying on others.

In 1850, with the aid and approval of the Presbyterian Church, the Elgin Settlement was born. Life was not easy for the original settlers, but they were very willing to teach newcomers the skills needed to succeed. There was a strict rule, however, that they did not give food, supplies, or clothing away. Pride in their own work, self-reliance, and independence were important goals. They were necessary for the success of the community and those who lived in it.

Education was the most important priority. With this in mind a school, open to all, was opened in 1850. It was not long before the Buxton school was better than the other schools in the region. Everyone, white and African, wanted to attend. By 1854, half of the students who attended the Buxton Mission school were white, even though all the teachers were African. Students at the school learned at a remarkable pace and all were taught subjects that included the Greek and Latin languages.

As the community grew, its settlers gained the respect of their white neighbours from nearby Chatham. They were known for their hard work and good business sense.

With the start of the American Civil War, however, changes to the Elgin Settlement began to take place. Many of the men returned to the United States and joined the Union (northern) army. The flow of people away could not be stopped, and the community became smaller and less prosperous.

The long-term effect of the Elgin Settlement was to prove that a self-supporting African community could exist in Canada. This was at a time when many whites doubted the abilities of the former slaves.

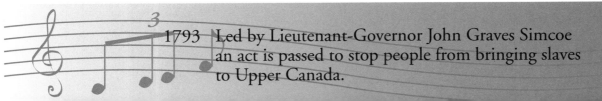

1793 Led by Lieutenant-Governor John Graves Simcoe an act is passed to stop people from bringing slaves to Upper Canada.

15

Activity: *Redesign Your Community*

Using the map on page 11 as an example, draw a map of your own community highlighting such focal points as your home, schools, grocery store, and so on.

If you were your community planner, how would you redesign the community? What parts would you change, and what parts would you keep? Explain why.

_____

_____

_____

_____

_____

_____

Saint John, New Brunswick

The history of Africans in New Brunswick dates back to the 1780s. Three groups of settlers were: former slaves who were brought by the United Empire Loyalists, free African people, and those who came as refugees after the War of 1812 between Canada and the United States.

Due to its location as a port and also its closeness to the United States border, Saint John became an important site and was a recognized terminal on the Underground Railroad.

Africans settled in all areas of the province originally, but, over time, those communities with larger populations attracted more and more people. The community of Saint John grew in size to where almost 50 per cent of the African population in the province lived there.

Most of the African people in Saint John worked as servants and labourers as they were very rarely able to find other jobs. One individual who did emerge as a leader in the early 1900s was Abraham B. Walker. He was a lawyer by education who also published a paper called the *Neith*. The paper was described as not being either a black or a white paper but a Canadian paper designed on the principles of liberty and equality for everyone.

The racism faced by the Africans in other areas in Canada was also found in New Brunswick. In churches they could sit only in the balcony, restaurants refused to serve them, and separate schools were common.

Through all this, however, Saint John, one of Canada's original settlement areas for those escaping slavery, has remained an important community in the story and history of Africans in Canada.

1813   A group of Africans from the Niagara area forms a militia company to defend Upper Canada from invasion by the United States.

Oro, Ontario

The Oro Settlement, near Barrie, Ontario, was founded in 1819 as a site able to protect Upper Canada from possible invasion from the United States.

Among the original settlers were 19 members of various militia units including Captain Runchey's Colored Corps. In 1827 Africans from Ohio and other areas moved into the community. It was hoped that the area would become a safe haven for escaped slaves.

As in other communities, white settlers received more (80 hectares) and better land, while the African Canadians had to accept land that was usually half the size and too rocky to farm.

With the poor land they were given, many had to work as farm hands for their white neighbours in order to support themselves and their families.

As they attempted to earn a living, the Africans in many cases were forced to sell sectors of their property. Lieutenant-Governor Sir John Colburne wanted to bring more white settlers into the area. He encouraged the sale of land, making the African community more isolated. As the sales increased, more of the African settlers began to look to other parts of the province in which to make their homes. A few families did try to hold on, but early in the 1900s the last of the community disappeared.

A monument in the town of Edgar with the names of Oro's original families is all that remains of this community.

Activity: *Write a Story*

Using the secret signs and the codes of the Underground Railroad write a story of how you made your escape from slavery to one of the communities you have just read about See how many of the signs and codes you can use in your story.

The Secret Language of Escape
Underground Railroad Codes

Agents, Conductors—people who aided escapees

Baggage, Package, Parcel—fugitive slaves, escapees

Black Grapevine—means of communication among slaves

Canaan, Heaven—Canada

Chariot—Underground Railroad

Drinking Gourd—North Star

Forwarding—leading escapees from station to station

Friend—Underground Railroad supporter; member of the Quaker faith

Lines—routes of escape

Market—Underground Railroad, abolitionist movement

Masons—secret "brotherhood" still operating today; secret handshakes were used to identify agents and passengers

Middle Passage—voyage across the Atlantic Ocean from freedom in Africa to slavery in the Americas

Moses—Harriet Tubman

Operator, Pilot—conductor, agent

Paddy rollers, Patrollers—slave catchers

Passenger—fugitive slave

Promised Land—before 1850, the northern states; after 1850, Canada

Refugees—escaping slaves

Shepherds—people who aided escapees

Slave Stealer—anyone (including the escaping slave) aiding escape

Soldier—fugitive slave

Stations—hiding places (usually homes along route)

Stationmasters—people who sheltered escapees

Stockholders—contributors of food, clothing, farm equipment, or money used for Underground Railroad cause

Terminal—final destination, safety

Tracks—back country trails

Trains—farm wagons with false bottoms used for escape

"The wind blows from the south today"—notice to Underground Railroad personnel of arriving escapees

Secret Signs of Escape

Log cabin quilt hanging outside porch—Underground Railroad station. The strong contrast of light/dark pattern pieces stood out from a distance

Black jockey in red cap, one extended hand holding lantern—Underground Railroad station

Boats in the night with hanging lights, a yellow one below a blue—Underground Railroad agents forwarding passengers along the line

Weather vanes—Route marker. The arrow of the weather vane pointed the direction for passengers on the road

"Faithful Groomsman" lantern bearer statue—Underground Railroad station. A light in the lantern signalled welcome; unlighted, meant danger

1821 The first Baptist church is established in Colchester County, Nova Scotia.

19

Amber Valley, Alberta

In the late 1800s Africans in America were actively encouraged by the Canadian government to settle in the West. The promise of free land and a chance to escape prejudice and discrimination attracted many former slaves

Alberta was the area where the majority of homesteading former African slaves and free people that went West decided to establish homes.

The Amber Valley area, north of Edmonton, became the largest rural community and the only one made up totally of African settlers. The area was first settled around 1909 by families from Oklahoma. Many decided to come to Canada when that state passed a law that took away African Americans' right to vote.

The settlers had to adjust very quickly to their new surroundings and the harsh climate. The challenges they faced were enormous. In their first winter the temperature dropped to −50°C. The land they settled had never been farmed. Like the white homesteaders who settled in the West, the people had to depend on themselves to supply their own food. The homesteads (farms) had large gardens in which everything possible was grown.

The strong farming history developed by their ancestors is still found in Amber Valley. A group of approximately 45 first- and second-generation descendants of the original settlers still call the community home, carrying on the work of the early pioneers.

Saltspring Island, British Columbia

In the 1850s African Americans arrived in the district that became British Columbia. The settlers who made the journey for the most part came from California. They were seeking a place free from the racism they had always had to endure.

The pioneer spirit of people like Louis and Sylvia Stark led to the creation of African communities on Saltspring Island, east of Vancouver Island. Originally it was an area where a few different nationalities of people settled. However, many of the first white settlers gave up their land claims after one winter owing to the severe conditions. For the new Africans in Canada the freedom they enjoyed outweighed the hardship. They did well enough to bring their families to the island.

In some early communities in Canada the people were kept segregated. On Saltspring, however, African and white settlers lived in the same communities. As the island became developed the numbers of whites on the island soon began to outnumber the African Canadian settlers.

Many of the problems such as racism that arose in other communities were not encountered to the same level on Saltspring Island. Prejudice was something neither group could afford to let happen. The help of a neighbour often meant survival, so racism could have proven very dangerous.

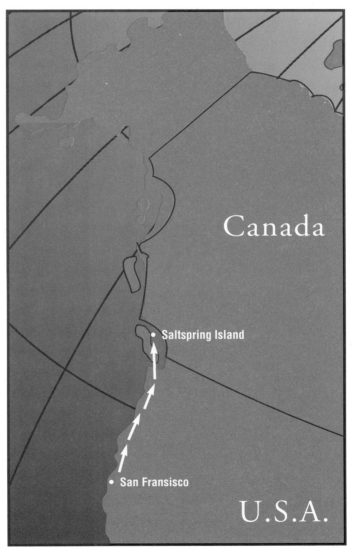

1834   The British Parliament abolishes slavery throughout its colonies and territories.

21

Africville, Nova Scotia

Africville was a community on the shore of the Bedford Basin close to Halifax. It was founded by descendants of refugees from the War of 1812. The pioneers had originally settled in other African communities such as Hammonds Plains and Preston. However, these places were too far for the people to travel easily to Halifax for work. The original settlers had hopes the new location would provide job opportunities.

As in other African Canadian communities, the people took great pride in themselves. They developed businesses, a school, and church as the centre of a strong community. However, this was not enough.

The people of Africville soon gave up their hopes of jobs in the city, and the community found itself increasingly isolated. City dumps and disposal pits people did not want in the white areas were placed dangerously close to the community and its homes. The residents of Africville were forced to accept living conditions well below the standards of other residents of Halifax. The unfair situation became even more obvious as time went on. The residents had to pay taxes to the City of Halifax for services that were never provided, such as indoor plumbing.

The injustice suffered by the people of the community reached its worst level beginning in 1962. The people were forced to move and their community was destroyed, because the city wanted the land. Further disrespect was shown when proper moving trucks were not provided to move the people. The city sent garbage trucks for their belongings.

A community dating back over 100 years, which, despite the hardships, provided great pride to those who lived there, was bulldozed forever. The last resident of Africville, Aaron "Pa" Carvery was forced out in January 1970.

For many former residents the move away from the historical community has been damaging. Many have suffered great hardships in their efforts to adjust.

The memory of Africville remains a modern example of the level of racism suffered by many Africans in Canada throughout history.

Activity: *Express Your Feelings*

Pretend you are Pa Carvery, the last person forced to leave Africville. Write a letter to the local newspaper telling your feelings about what has happened to your community.

Pa Carvery

1837   The Anti-Slavery Society of Canada is organized to try to abolish slavery across North America.

23

Activity: *Locate the Communities*

1. On the map of Canada provided, place the locations of the historic communities you have read about.
2. Can you identify any other African Canadian communities, past or present, that you can add to the map. (Your parent or teacher may need to help you discover the hidden history around you.)

Canada

0   500   1000 km

Music and Its Meaning

Like Africans all over the world, African Canadians come from a continent where music—including song and dance—is an important part of life. It has been used both in times of celebration and in times of sadness.

The unique rhythms and sounds of Africa now heard around the world have been passed down from our ancestors to us today.

During the growth of the slave trade, Africans were captured and brought to North America (along with other areas). Many converted to Christianity after their arrival in the New World. It was from those who held them captive that they learned religious songs to which they added African beats and melodies. They also created songs to relate stories from homes left behind or to send messages among the hostages.

The songs that developed were named spirituals because they often dealt with religious subjects and because they expressed the spirit of oppressed people who wished to be set free from the chains of slavery. The songs became a source of hope and a method of keeping spirits high.

The story of how Moses led the Hebrew people out of slavery was used as the theme of many songs to express the people's wish to be free. The songs were chanted in the fields while the Africans worked and in slave cabins while they rested. Spirituals were also sung at secret meetings where the captives planned their escapes north to what was known as "The Freedom Land" or back to Africa, which was known as "The Other Shore."

To the many Africans escaping north by using the Underground Railroad, song and music were very important either to warn of danger or to send messages of success.

Music spread along the entire route to freedom and has been used by Africans in North America as a common bond at various times in history.

25

The Evolution of African Music in North America

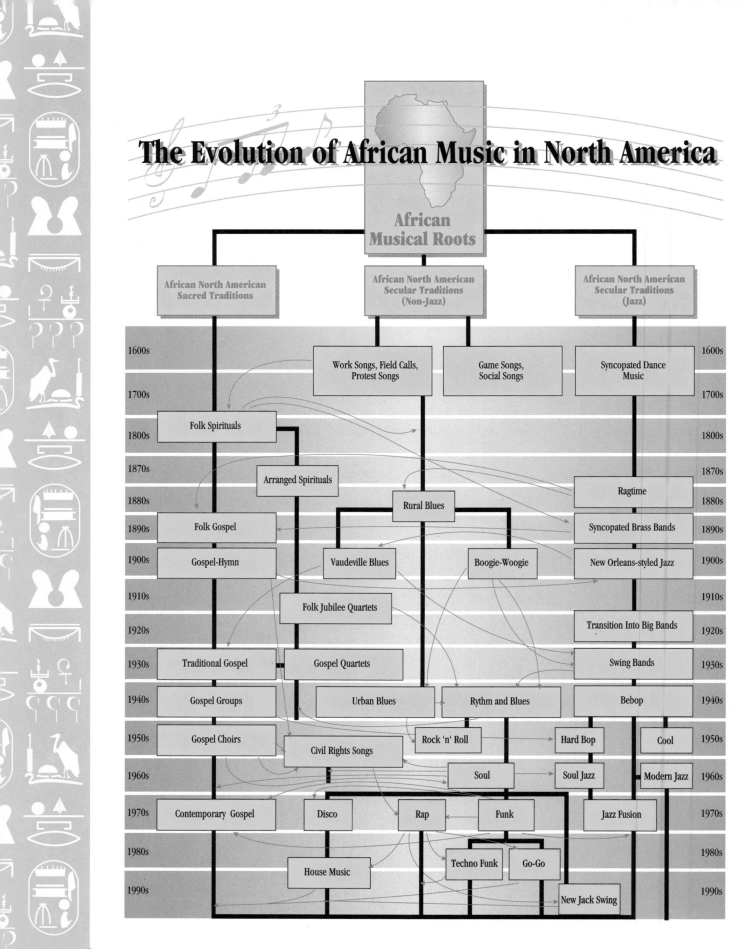

African Musical Roots

African North American Sacred Traditions	African North American Secular Traditions (Non-Jazz)	African North American Secular Traditions (Jazz)

1600s	Work Songs, Field Calls, Protest Songs — Game Songs, Social Songs	Syncopated Dance Music	**1600s**
1700s			**1700s**
1800s	Folk Spirituals		**1800s**
1870s	Arranged Spirituals	Ragtime	**1870s**
1880s	Rural Blues		**1880s**
1890s	Folk Gospel	Syncopated Brass Bands	**1890s**
1900s	Gospel-Hymn — Vaudeville Blues — Boogie-Woogie	New Orleans-styled Jazz	**1900s**
1910s	Folk Jubilee Quartets		**1910s**
1920s		Transition Into Big Bands	**1920s**
1930s	Traditional Gospel — Gospel Quartets	Swing Bands	**1930s**
1940s	Gospel Groups — Urban Blues — Rythm and Blues	Bebop	**1940s**
1950s	Gospel Choirs — Civil Rights Songs — Rock 'n' Roll — Hard Bop	Cool	**1950s**
1960s	Soul — Soul Jazz	Modern Jazz	**1960s**
1970s	Contemporary Gospel — Disco — Rap — Funk — Jazz Fusion		**1970s**
1980s	House Music — Techno Funk — Go-Go		**1980s**
1990s	New Jack Swing		**1990s**

CAUTION

Materials
glue (white)
hand drill with twist drill bit
popsicle sticks (four)
wood: scrap blocks and thin strips
pencil
ruler
sandpaper
screwdriver
screws, roundhead (two)

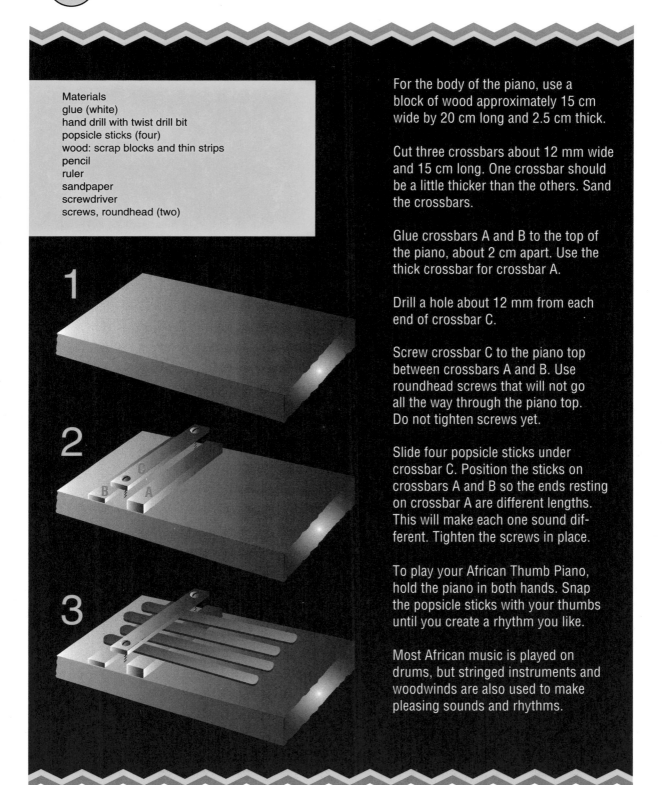

For the body of the piano, use a block of wood approximately 15 cm wide by 20 cm long and 2.5 cm thick.

Cut three crossbars about 12 mm wide and 15 cm long. One crossbar should be a little thicker than the others. Sand the crossbars.

Glue crossbars A and B to the top of the piano, about 2 cm apart. Use the thick crossbar for crossbar A.

Drill a hole about 12 mm from each end of crossbar C.

Screw crossbar C to the piano top between crossbars A and B. Use roundhead screws that will not go all the way through the piano top. Do not tighten screws yet.

Slide four popsicle sticks under crossbar C. Position the sticks on crossbars A and B so the ends resting on crossbar A are different lengths. This will make each one sound different. Tighten the screws in place.

To play your African Thumb Piano, hold the piano in both hands. Snap the popsicle sticks with your thumbs until you create a rhythm you like.

Most African music is played on drums, but stringed instruments and woodwinds are also used to make pleasing sounds and rhythms.

Sheet Music

Siyahamb'e

Arr. by Woody Woods

With an easy swaying motion, not too fast

Zulu Song

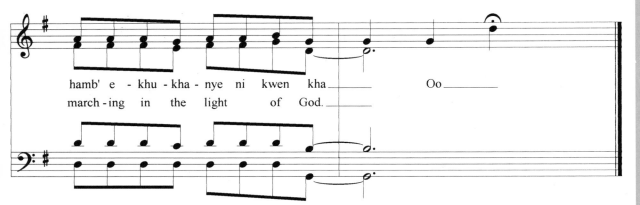

hamb' e - khu - kha - nye ni kwen kha_____ Oo_____
march -ing in the light of God._____

30

Lift Ev'ry Voice And Sing

Arr. by Woody Woods

J. W. Johnson
J. R. Johnson

Lift Ev'ry Voice And Sing - pg. 3

33

34

Color Me Love

35

Just A Closer Walk With Thee

Arr. by Woody Woods

Dai - ly walk - ing close to Thee,

let it be, Dear

Lord, let it be.

Just A Closer Walk With Thee - pg. 3

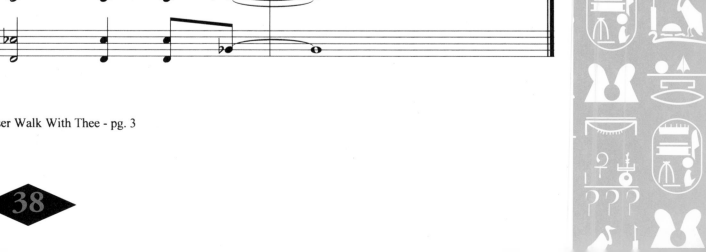

38

Let Us Break Bread Together

Traditional

Let us break bread to-get-her on our
Let us praise God to-get-her on our

knees. _____ Let us break bread to -
knees. _____ Let us praise God to -

get-her on ___ our knees. On ___ our knees. When I
get-her on ___ our knees. On ___ our knees.

39

Kum Ba Yah

Arr. by Woody Woods

We Are A Family

Woody Woods

We are a fam - ily, u - ni - ted we stand, di - vid - ed we fall.

G   D/E   D   G⁷

We are a fam - ily, all for one one for all.

Cmaj⁷   Am⁷   D⁷

We are a fam - ily, u - ni - ted we stand, di - vid - ed we fall.

G D/E D G⁷

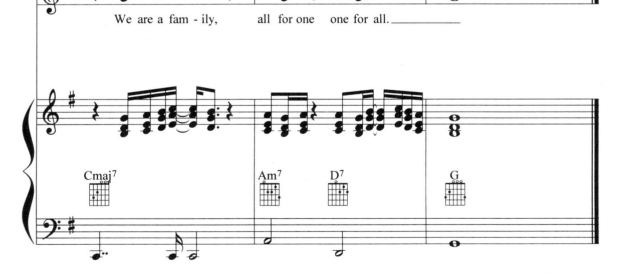

We are a fam - ily, all for one   one for all._____

Cmaj⁷ Am⁷ D⁷ G

We Are A Family - pg. 2

43

I Need You, Lord

Slowly with feeling

Woody Woods

Learn To Dream

Slowly with feeling

Woody Woods

With - out a dream in your heart you're lost from the start. You'll ne-ver get to where you want to

go. If you for - get how to feel, then no - thing is real, and

no - thing's all you're e - ver gon-na know. If your life is turned a - bout, filled with

48

A Song of My Own

Woody Woods

Activity: *Write a Song*

Write your own lyrics for the piece of music on page 50 called *A Song of My Own*.
It is the last track on the cassette tape that came with this book.

Achievement

African Canadians continue to make great strides in Canadian society. Like Mattieu da Costa in 1605 who conducted the trading between Samuel de Champlain and the Mi'kmaq people, African Canadians have excelled in many different professions.

The search for equality by Africans in North America is over 300 years old. Each new generation has produced leaders and role models who have advanced the search a little further. No matter how different their origins, all our role models continue to provide evidence that achievement is possible in our time.

From the struggle and cruelty suffered by hostages after being stolen from the shores of Africa to the efforts of African Americans and others at the forefront of the Civil Rights Movements of the 1960s, tomorrow's leaders can look to the efforts of current African Canadians who continue to break new ground.

The achievers you will read about are just a few of many throughout Canada. Others are equally deserving of recognition.

Activity: *Conduct an Interview*

Using the biographies that follow as your guide, conduct an interview with someone in your community or family that you admire. It may be interesting to talk to someone who has moved from another country. What other questions might you ask to discover information about this person?

_____

_____

_____

_____

_____

_____

_____

_____

_____

1841   Rev. Josiah Henson, an escaped slave, helps set up the British-American Institute, a place where other refugees could study and live, at the Dawn Settlement (now Dresden, Ont.).

Howard McCurdy

Dr. McCurdy is known throughout Canada as someone who stands up for the rights of the individual. His work has led him from the classroom to the Parliament of Canada, never once giving up on his vision and hope of a society built on equality.

Q Where were you born?

A I was born in London, Ontario.

Q Who were your role models?

A My parents and family were my main role models. We can trace back seven generations to approximately 1830.

Q Did you have any hobbies?

A The hobbies I had included reading, drawing, and inventing things. I was very science oriented but also enjoyed learning about history as well as participating in sports such as baseball, basketball, and track and field.

Q What did you wish to be when you were growing up? Why?

A I originally wanted to be a baseball player or a doctor. I thought those would be interesting professions.

Q If you could send a message to African Canadian children, what would it be?

A They are just as capable as anybody else. The same things that make us good athletes, such as talent, motivation, discipline, and intellect, can make you a success in any field. Racism is not a wall but a distraction that can make you lose sight of your goal.

Q Has racism ever touched you, and how did you deal with it?

A I first really noticed racism at the age of nine. I saw there was a colour consciousness among Black people and that we were excluded from things by many white people. I had a strong sense of racial pride. I was determined to fight injustice from an early age.

Q How large was your family when you were growing up?

A There are two children, my sister and I.

Q Did you and your sister get along?

A We got along as well as any kids in a family get along.

Q Was the push to succeed strong in all the family?

A Success was something that the whole family tried to attain. With the strong history we had of prominent individuals, it was natural to expect a lot from our efforts.

Q What did you learn about Black history when you were growing up?

A My mother tried to always teach us about our roots. That we all came from great African kings and queens. The fact that my family could trace back to being guides (or conductors) on the Underground Railroad and our family connection with Delos Davis, the first Black King's Counsel [lawyer] in Ontario and other important historical figures was taught to us.

Q Did you ever feel separate and different from the other students because of your colour and heritage?

A Yes I felt different but more often than not I felt that my heritage made me special.

Q What was your favourite subject in school?

A Chemistry.

Q What is your favourite colour?

A Blue.

Q What is/was your favourite vegetable?

A Potatoes.

Q What were your parents' occupations?

A My mother worked with the public service in community services for many years. My father worked at few different things, usually holding two jobs at a time. His work included things like being a carpenter, a plumber, and a plant supervisor.

Education

I graduated from Assumption College with my Bachelor of Arts and Bachlor of Science, I then went to Michigan State where I completed my Masters and Ph.D. in Biochemistry and Microbiology.

Achievements

- Member of Parliament for Windsor
- President, Canadian Association of University Teachers
- Head of the Biology Department—University of Windsor
- Founding President, National Black Coalition

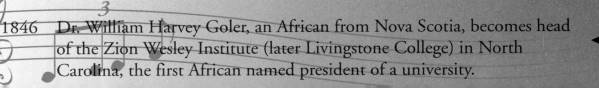

1846 Dr. William Harvey Goler, an African from Nova Scotia, becomes head of the Zion Wesley Institute (later Livingstone College) in North Carolina, the first African named president of a university.

Lincoln Alexander

Lincoln Alexander has been recognized as a leader for many years. As the first African Canadian Member of Parliament, federal cabinet minister, and Lieutenant Governor, he is a modern-day pioneer.

Q   Where were you born?

A   I was born in Toronto but spent part of my youth growing up in New York City.

Q   Who were your role models?

A   I didn't really have any role models. I always believed in myself and tried to search for personal excellence.

Q   Did you have any hobbies?

A   My main hobbies were sports like soccer, softball, and lacrosse along with other typical things kids do.

Q   What did you wish to be when you were growing up? Why?

A   I didn't really have a idea on what I wanted to be. I knew that I liked school and that my mother always said to me that I had to continue it because education was the key to my future.

Q   If you could send a message to African Canadian children, what would it be?

A   Life is not easy, but you can be a productive part of society. Education will unlock a lot of doors. Help yourself by recognizing this and strive for more. Being Black alone will not be able to be used as an excuse for lack of opportunities. Strive to be above average and the best you can possibly be.

Q   Has racism ever touched you and how did you deal with it?

A   Racism will always be a part of my life. It has led to many conflicts that as a child my confidence in myself helped me to overcome.

Q   How large was your family when you were growing up?

A   There were two children, both boys.

Q   Did you and your brother get along?

A   This was difficult, as my youth was spent in a separated family, and we did not live together.

Q   Was the push to succeed strong in all the family?

A   No, the push was to be educated and from there things would take care of themselves.

Q   What did you learn about Black history when you were growing up?

A   Not very much. However, I think the motivation should be to learn about all histories in order to make a truly knowledgeable person.

Q   Did you ever feel separate and different from the other students because of your colour and heritage?

A   I didn't feel separate, because I always knew who I was. What others thought of me was their own concern. I knew I was Black in a white neighbourhood, but I didn't spend any time worrying about it.

Q   What was your favourite subject in school?

A   I always liked geography as a subject, but more so I enjoyed the school experience because of the friendships I developed.

Q   What is/was your favourite colour?

A   Dark blue seems to be the colour I have always been partial to.

Q   What is/was your favourite vegetable?

A   Spinach was my favourite.

Q   What were your parents' occupations?

A   My mother worked as a domestic (housekeeper); my father was a railroad porter.

Education
Graduate of McMaster University and Osgoode Hall Law School

Achievements
• Chancellor of the University of Guelph
• Lieutenant-Governor of Ontario 1985–91
• Companion of the Order of Canada
• Member of the Order of Ontario
• Man of the Year Award—Ethnic Press Council of Canada
• John G. Diefenbaker Memorial Foundation Canadian Award
• First African Canadian elected to the House of Commons (MP for Hamilton West, 1968)
• Former Federal Minister of Labour (1970)

1859   Led by John Brown, abolitionists attack Harpers Ferry, West Virginia. The attack is believed to have been planned while Brown was staying at the home of African Canadian poet James Madison Bell in Chatham, Ontario.

Emery Barnes

As the Speaker of the British Columbia Legislature and its longest-sitting member, this former professional football player has shown the same determination in serving the community as he displayed on the field.

Q Where were you born?

A I was born in New Orleans, Louisiana, USA, but I spent part of my youth in Hermiston and Portland, Oregon.

Q Who were your role models?

A I looked up to a number of people. There was a schoolmate of mine named John Freeman. He was an outstanding athlete and someone whom I greatly admired. Another role model was Mr. Edwin Barry, former President of the Portland (Oregon) Urban League. As a counsellor he kept me out of trouble at a point in my young life (16 years old) when I was most vulnerable and easily led astray. Isobelle Gates, a white community activist, encouraged me to join Portland's first interracial choir. There was Joe Lewis, world champion fighter, and Paul Robeson and Marian Anderson, great singers.

Q Did you have any hobbies?

A Usually I hung around with my small circle of friends. I always did like music, but by age 13 I decided I would like to try athletics.

Q What did you wish to be when you were growing up? Why?

A I didn't really have any clear picture of what I wanted to be. After I found out I was a pretty good athlete, I began thinking that I would like to make sports my profession. As for why, I just wanted to be someone who was appreciated, respected, loved, and valued by others.

Q If you could send a message to African Canadian children, what would it be?

A Dreams of hope can come true if you keep a clear vision of where you are going. Think positive and work through the ups and downs in life; believe in yourself. Learning should be a life-long experience, so keep an open mind.

Q Has racism ever touched you and how did you deal with it?

A Yes I have had to deal with racism. My first feelings of vulnerability to racism were felt at a very early age. In the Southern USA at that time, Blacks were forced by law to accept less than white people. This not only made me aware of my race and colour; I also asked questions like what were the reasons and the thinking that created such an inhumane and unfair system.

Q How large was your family when you were growing up?

A I have an older sister; counting my mother, we were three.

Q Did you and your sister get along?

A We were very close. While we were growing up, my sister became my primary defender and protector. She had a way of handling bullies who were after me—she could be awesome.

Q Was the push to succeed strong in all the family?

A My mother's example of hard work, responsibility, duty, and unwavering will impressed me at an early age, and I learned much by her example and her determination.

Q What did you learn about Black history when you were growing up?

A I learned very little about Black history while in public school or when I went to university. As an adult I've have made an effort to inform myself by collecting information wherever I could find it.

Q Did you ever feel separate and different from the other students because of your colour and heritage?

A Yes, you see I grew up in a time when segregation between Blacks and Whites was the norm. But it wasn't very long before I realized that racism was a mean sword that cut both ways. Its perpetrators suffered as much as its targets.

Q What was your favourite subject in school?

A My favourite subjects were music, art, and sports—human relations.

Q What is/was your favourite colour?

A In high school it was royal blue. Today it's the rainbow.

Q What is/was your favourite vegetable?

A I loved peas, tomatoes, greens, and cabbage. Vegetables were usually grown in our yard and formed the main part of my family's diet.

Q What were your parents' occupations?

A I was raised solely by my mother. She was a housekeeper and usually held at least two jobs. Later she went back to school and trained to become a practical nurse.

Education

After graduating high school in Portland, I went on to receive my Bachelor of Science degree from the University of Oregon. I later attended the University of British Columbia where I received a Bachelor of Social Work degree.

Achievements

- Speaker of the Legislative Assembly, Province of British Columbia
- Elected six times to the British Columbia legislature
- Member of the 1952 U.S. Olympic Team and All-American high jumper
- Member of the B.C. Lions 1964 Grey Cup Championship Team
- Recipient of the Silver Anniversary Award at the University of Oregon as its Most Outstanding Athlete for a 25-year period.

1861 Dr. Anderson Ruffin Abbot becomes the first Canadian-born Black to graduate from medical school. (See Vol. I in this series, *Out of the Past Into the Future.*)

Rosemary Brown

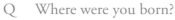

Rosemary Brown was the first African
Canadian woman to be elected
to the British Columbia legislature.
As Chief Commissioner of the
Ontario Human Rights
Commission, she continues her
life-long dedication to fighting injustice.

Q   Where were you born?

A   I was born in Kingston, Jamaica.

Q   Who were your role models?

A   Nanny of the Maroons, who was a female who led an uprising against slavery in Jamaica, was one role model. Others would be Norman Manley, who was an important person who fought for Jamaican independence, and my grandmother, Imo James. She fought for adult suffrage.

Q   Did you have any hobbies?

A   Reading was my main hobby, because as a child there was no TV. Playing piano was another hobby.

Q   What did you wish to be when you were growing up? Why?

A   I wanted to be a famous courtroom lawyer because I was always impressed by people who could use words. Lawyers were the great orators in Jamaica at the time.

Q   If you could send a message to African Canadian children, what would it be?

A   I would want the children to know race can be a catalyst rather than an obstacle. It should be what spurs you on to be the best you can be rather than an obstacle and an excuse for failure. The choice of how you see yourself is your own.

Q   Has racism ever touched you and how did you deal with it?

A   I have lived with it every day of my life. It became more obvious upon my moving to Canada.

Q   How large was your family when you were growing up?

A   One brother and one sister.

Q   Did you and your siblings get along?

A   We behaved like normal children.

Q   Was the push to succeed strong in all the family?

A   We were raised primarily by my grandmother. High achievement was expected of all the kids. There was no question of us not going to university and doing the best we could possibly do.

Q   What did you learn about Black history when you were growing up?

A   When I was in school we did learn Jamaican history but nothing about Africa. Anything I learned about Africa was passed onto me by relatives who had lived there.

Q   What was your favourite subject in school?

A   My favourite subject was literature.

Q   What is/was your favourite colour?

A   My favourite colour was/is red.

Q   What is/was your favourite vegetable?

A   My favourite vegetable was either plantain or breadfruit.

Education

I graduated from McGill University in Montreal and then went on to obtain my Masters Degree from the University of British Columbia in Vancouver.

Achievements

• The United Nations Fellowship
• National Black Coalition Award

1863   The Emancipation Proclamation is passed in the United States, abolishing slavery.

Willie O'Ree

Willie O'Ree is known as the Jackie Robinson of hockey. This native of New Brunswick broke that sport's colour barrier in 1958 when he first took to the ice for the Boston Bruins. His life story is told in the documentary film *Echoes in the Rink: The Willie O'Ree Story.*

Q   Where were you born?

A   I was born and raised in Fredericton, New Brunswick.

Q   Who were your role models?

A   I didn't really have any role models, but someone I greatly admired was Jackie Robinson (first Black player in major league base-ball—Brooklyn Dodgers 1947).

Q   Did you have any hobbies?

A   Sports were always my main hobbies. I started skating when I was three and began organized hockey at age five.

Q   What did you wish to be when you were growing up?

A   I wanted to be an athlete of some sort. I played hockey in the winter and baseball in the summer. I was lucky and had enough talent that in 1952 the Milwaukee Braves [major league baseball team] invited me to attend one of their tryout camps in Georgia. My heart really was not in it, however, as hockey was my first love.

Q   If you could send a message to African Canadian children, what would it be?

A   If you pick something you wish to do, excel in it. Many doors have been opened, and while you will still have to make some sacrifices and things may get difficult, you have to work harder to do the best that you can do.

Q   Has racism ever touched you and how did you deal with it?

A   I never really noticed it until I was a little older. When I started playing midget hockey the name calling became more obvious. I dealt with it by deciding I could either let it get to me or work to be that much better than everybody else. I made it a point that any team I tried out for, I made, and the level of competition didn't matter.

Q   How large was your family when you were growing up?

A   There were seven children in our family. I was the youngest with four sisters and two brothers.

Q   Did you and your siblings get along?

A   The family was very close. The O'Ree family, while being one of only two Black families in Fredericton, was quite a prominent one, because of the efforts and name the kids made for themselves in various sports.

Q   Was the push to succeed strong in all the family?

A   The push to succeed was strong. I decided to prove to myself and the people of Fredericton I could do something better than anyone else.

Q   What did you learn about Black history when you were growing up?

A   There were only two or three Black children in the school I attended, and there was never any real history taught to us. It just wasn't a priority for the schools. I knew some basic family history that was told to me by my parents and grandparents.

Q   Did you ever feel separate and different from the other students because of your colour and heritage?

A   I always knew I was Black, but while I may have felt different, I always had a group of friends that I grew up with that always made me part of the group. These were kids that I mostly played on teams with.

Q   What was your favourite subject in school?

A   Math and social studies were my favourite subjects.

Q   What is/was your favourite colour?

A   Blues and brown.

Q   What is/was your favourite vegetable?

A   Potatoes and broccoli.

Q   What were your parents' occupations?

A   My mother was a homemaker and stayed at home. My father worked for the maintenance and engineering department for the City of Fredericton.

Achievements
• First Black player in the National Hockey League
• Member of New Brunswick Sports Hall of Fame
• Member of the Hall of Champions in San Diego, California

1870   John Hamilton, an employee with the New Brunswick Railway Land Company, invents the first railway flanger, used to keep rails free of snow and slush.

63

Charmaine Crooks

Since the early 1980s,
Charmaine Crooks has risen to the top
as one of the world's fastest sprinters, through hard work and
dedication to fair play. She is a television host for the CBC and is involved in
public speaking along with her work as a sports commentator.

Q   Where were you born?

A   I was born in St. Elizabeth, Jamaica, and moved to Canada at age five.

Q   Who were your role models?

A   My mother was my main role model, she was a very strong influence.

Q   Did you have any hobbies?

A   I loved writing poetry, and I was also involved in many different sports.

Q   What did you wish to be when you were growing up?

A   I had always wanted to be a teacher and work with children.

Q   If you could send a message to African Canadian children what would it be?

A   I want the children to be part of your community, get involved. It's your world, so take part in it and never give up on your dream.

Q   Has racism ever touched you, and how did you deal with it?

A   I was brought up to believe that if someone had a problem with me because of my colour, it was their problem, not mine. I wouldn't let myself be intimidated and stopped from doing the things I wanted to take part in.

Q   How large was your family when you were growing up?

A   There were seven children in my family, four girls and three boys.

Q   Did you and your siblings get along?

A   We all got along very well.

Q   Was the push to succeed strong in all the family?

A   We were all encouraged to work hard. Education was very important.

Q   What did you learn about Black history when you were growing up?

A   I didn't learn much about Black history. The one real experience I had was visiting the Harriet Tubman Centre in Toronto.

Q   Did you ever feel separate and different from the other students because of your colour and heritage?

A   I always felt I was an individual and made my own choices. Being an athlete really stressed that to me. While I didn't feel different because of my colour or heritage, I felt the difference in how I was going to live my life. It was easy to make choices like staying away from drugs because it would have hurt my running.

Q   What was your favourite subject in school?

A   The things I enjoyed most were reading and writing.

Q   What is/was your favourite colour?

A   Red and yellow.

Q   What is/was your favourite vegetable?

A   I like all vegetables, from the traditional things in Canada to things like yams and akee from Jamaica.

Q   What were your parents' occupations?

A   My father worked as a welder for the Ford Motor Company. My mother worked part-time for Sears.

Education

I graduated from West Toronto High School and went to the University of Texas at El Paso on an athletic scholarship. I studied psychology at university.

Achievements
- Numerous national and international atheletic awards
- Silver medal at the 1984 Olympics as a member of the 4 x 4 relay team
- Recipient of the Canada 125 Medal for Citizenship

1880   Mary Ann Shadd (Cary), fighting for equal rights for women, organizes the Colored Women's Progressive Association.

65

Beverly Mascoll

Never doubting her ability, she has built Canada's largest Africa Canadian cosmetic company. Her hard work and dedication are proof that an idea is never too large and no goals are out of reach.

Q Where were you born?

A I was born in Dartmouth, Nova Scotia.

Q Who were your role models?

A I was very fortunate to have four role models: my mother, my grandmother, a family friend, Mrs. Ada Lee, and a teacher, Selena Jefferson.

Q Did you have any hobbies?

A I played a lot outdoors doing normal kid's activities. A favourite game of mine was to pretend I was in business selling things.

Q What did you wish to be when you were growing up? Why?

A I always thought being a dietician would be an interesting job, but I'm glad I focused on business instead.

Q If you could send a message to African Canadian children, what would it be?

A I would want all the kids to have high self-esteem. To assist in gaining that esteem our youth should seek out role models either in their families or outside. Pattern your efforts after someone who has succeeded, and don't be afraid to approach that adult and ask for some direction.

Q Has racism ever touched you and how did you deal with it?

A Yes it has. I grew up in a community which was mainly white. Being the only African Canadian children in the school, racism was all around us.

An example of this was during assembly songs such as *Old Black Joe* and others would be sung. The other kids would all look at us during these times.

There was a store contest involving sticks of gum. The idea was to get the black stick, which was called the "pickaninny stick." That was a very negative term directed specifically at Black children. Once I understood that it was a negative term, I made others aware of how I felt. I let them know that it offended me.

Q How large was your family when you were growing up?

A There were three children in the family, I have two brothers.

Q Did you and your brothers get along?

A We all got along—partially due to the fact we were the only African Canadian children in the town, so we tended to look out for one another.

Q Was the push to succeed strong in all the family?

A Not particularly. We were fairly independent.

Q What did you learn about Black history when you were growing up?

A Not very much at all. The history books made it seem like we didn't exist until slavery. It wasn't until I was an adult that I learned about the many contributions we have made.

Q Did you ever feel separate and different from the other students because of your colour and heritage?

A Yes, we felt different being the only African Canadians in town. People tried to make us feel as if we were different, but older family members let us know that nobody was any better or worse.

Q What was your favourite subject in school?

A Economics was a favourite course of mine as a teen.

Q What is/was your favourite colour?

A Red.

Q What is/was your favourite vegetable?

A Potato, whether I liked it or not, was a part of our diet.

Q What were your parents' occupations?

A My mother was a teacher, and my father worked for a construction company.

Education
After I graduated from technical school, I went directly to work as a businesswoman.

Achievements
• Recipient of the Harry Jerome Award for Business
• Member of the Black Cultural Centre of Nova Scotia's Wall of Honour
• Vice President of the Canadian Club
• YWCA, Woman of Distinction Award
• Canadian Black Achievement Award—Business
• Governor, University of Guelph Board of Governors

1882 John Ware, a cowboy, moves from Texas to Alberta. He became an important figure in the history of that province. (See Vol. I in this series, *Out of the Past Into the Future*.)

Lou Gannon

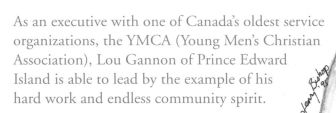

As an executive with one of Canada's oldest service organizations, the YMCA (Young Men's Christian Association), Lou Gannon of Prince Edward Island is able to lead by the example of his hard work and endless community spirit.

Q   Where were you born?

A   I was born in Halifax, Nova Scotia.

Q   Who were your role models?

A   Because I always wanted to be a professional athlete, my role models were usually star hockey players or basketball players.

Q   Did you have any hobbies?

A   My hobbies included basketball, swimming, and playing guitar.

Q   What did you wish to be when you were growing up? Why?

A   When I was young I always wanted to be a pilot. Because I did not give school the priority it deserved, I had to change my thinking.

Q   If you could send a message to African Canadian children, what would it be?

A   Everyone has skills and the effort should be in finding what your skills are. Being afraid of failing at something should not stop your efforts. Success comes at various stages of life, and our children should strive to continue to grow. Don't forget your roots.

Q   Has racism ever touched you and how did you deal with it?

A   I realized I was Black and different in the way people treated me.

Q   How large was your family when you were growing up?

A   There were eight children in our family, six boys and two girls.

Q   Did you and your siblings get along?

A   For the most part all the kids got along with each other.

Q   Was the push to succeed strong in all the family?

A   Our parents wanted all the children to have better opportunities than they had.

Q   What did you learn about Black history when you were growing up?

A   I learned or was taught nothing about Black history while growing up, it was in university that I first learned we had a history.

Q   Did you ever feel separate and different from the other students because of your colour and heritage?

A   I was fortunate that because I was a good athlete and musician most of the feelings of being different were positive. I could do things the other kids couldn't.

Q   What was your favourite subject in school?

A   My favourite subject in school was history. It was all European history, however. The only things I knew of Black people and their accomplishments was what was said in the media.

Q   What is/was your favourite colour?

A   My favourite colours were purple and grey.

Q   What is/was your favourite vegetable?

A   Corn on the cob.

Q   What were your parents' occupations?

A   My mother was a housekeeper, and my father worked for a time with the railroad.

Education:

I studied physical education while attending Dalhousie University.

Achievements

• First and only Black Chief Executive of a YMCA in Canada
• Member of the Canadian YMCA Urban Group
• Awarded in 1993 the Canada 125 Commemorative Medal in recognition of significant contribution to communities in Canada
• Member of the Canadian Youth Developing Agencies delegation to Russia in 1989

1885   Delos Rogest Davis of Amherstburg, is the first African Canadian lawyer admitted to the Law Society of Upper Canada. Because of racism, Davis had not been allowed to attend law school, so he taught himself.

Calvin Ruck

From his personal interest in African Canadian history, he has written the story of the No. 2 Construction Battalion (Canada's first and only Black battalion), which took part in World War I. He is continuing to research and bring to light other historical events that have shaped the lives of Africans in Canada.

Q   Where were you born?

A   I was born in Sydney, Nova Scotia. My parents were originally from Barbados in the West Indies.

Q   Who were your role models?

A   The main one I had as child was a gentleman named Mr. John Armstrong, a native of Barbados, who lived in our community. He was someone most of the young men could look up to and identify with. He always had time for the young people and just seemed to connect with us.

Q   Did you have any hobbies?

A   Sports were my main hobbies. I enjoyed things like softball and hockey. Those games were popular with almost everyone. We also played cricket.

Q   What did you wish to be when you were growing up? Why?

A   I didn't really have any goals. I just knew that at a certain time I would have to start working. Jobs around Sydney were largely based around the steel plant so that was always there.

Q   If you could send a message to African Canadian children, what would it be?

A   The young people today must strive to get a good education. Train for something, then reach for the top.

Q   Has racism ever touched you and how did you deal with it?

A   The community was racially mixed. I didn't really have any problems until I was older and able to understand it. The most obvious things we saw were that certain jobs were known to be ones not to apply for, because it was known Blacks wouldn't be hired.

Q   How large was your family when you were growing up?

A   There were five boys in our family.

Q   Did you and your siblings get along?

A   We got along as most kids do. The older ones directed the younger ones.

Q   Was the push to succeed strong in all the family?

A   The push to succeed and pursue excellence was not that strong. This was mainly due to the absence of our parents.

My mother died when I was 3, and my father when I was 11. We all had to leave school earlier than I'm sure they would have wanted.

Q   What did you learn about Black history when you were growing up?

A   We learned nothing. I didn't even hear the term Black history until I was an adult. The texts in schools didn't have any reference to our achievements at all. Africa was never portrayed in a positive fashion.

Q   Did you ever feel separate and different from the other students because of your colour and heritage?

A   The schools were integrated, so while I knew I was a different colour, there were a lot of various ethnic backgrounds we all had to accept and get along with. Also, because of the area I grew up in, everyone had the same basic standard of living. It was a working class community.

Q   What was your favourite subject in school?

A   History was always my favourite subject.

Q   What is/was your favourite colour?

A   I didn't really have a favourite colour.

Q   What is/was your favourite vegetable?

A   Cucumber—we didn't have it very often so it was a special treat.

Education

I dropped out of school in Grade 10 to go to work. I went back to school in 1977 by attending the Maritime School of Social Work where I obtained a Diploma in Social Work.

Achievements
- Harry Jerome Award, 1986
- Honorary Doctorate of Humanities from Dalhousie University
- Freda Vickery Award for community service from the Maritime School of Social Work
- Member of the Order of Canada

1904   Year of birth of African American doctor Charles Drew, who attended McGill University in Montreal and later invented the process for allowing blood to be stored.

Glenda Simms

As President of the Canadian Advisory Council on the Status of Women, Dr. Simms heads one of the most influential organizations in Canada. Its work to make an equal and fair society affected all Canadians.

Q   Where were you born?

A   I was born and raised in the District of Stanmore, Saint Elizabeth Parish, on the island of Jamaica.

Q   Who were your role models?

A   My main role model was a woman named Millicent Knight. She was the vice-principal of the Bethlehem Teachers' College. She was always a strong, positive person and she taught us to be positive about being Jamaican women.

Q   Did you have any hobbies?

A   I read a lot as a child, I was very interested in books. Another hobby was to explore nature, I was especially interested in wild flowers.

Q   What did you wish to be when you were growing up? Why?

A   The two main professions at that time for young girls were teaching and nursing. One of my early goals was that at some point in time I wished to be principal of the teachers' college. At the age of 18 I went to teachers' college. It was while there that I felt that I wanted to progress to be a university professor.

Q   If you could send a message to African Canadian children, what would it be?

A   I want all the children to grow up feeling good about themselves. Be proud to be African Canadian, love the texture of your hair, the colour and feel of your skin. We all come from an exciting past, and we have an exciting future. I also want them to be conscious of the negative feelings around them and set out to be the best they can possibly be.

Q   Has racism ever touched you and how did you deal with it?

A   As a child the racism I felt was quite unique. People in our community were very shade-conscious. The darker you were the less value you were given as a person. Because I was a very dark-skinned person I would always strive to be the best so I had to be accepted. My family always made me feel confident and taught me to be proud.

Q   How large was your family when you were growing up?

A   There were seven children, five girls and two boys.

Q   Did you and your siblings get along?

A   We were very close. Because there were four girls born at first, we all grew up learning to depend upon each other. When our brothers came along we took care of them and caused all of the children to have a role.

Q   Was the push to succeed strong in all the family?

A   Hard work was expected. My mother used to always say to us "you have to be a some-body."

Q   What did you learn about Black history when you were growing up?

A   I learned very little about African history. I was fortunate however to have the benefited from listening to people telling stories orally. The oral tradition was strong in the community, and because of my ancestors having lived there I got a strong sense of family traditions and history. As an adult I have learned more about our cultural history.

Q   Did you ever feel separate and different from the other students because of your colour and heritage?

A   Separate only because of the emphasis placed on what shade of brown your skin was.

Q   What was your favourite subject in school?

A   My favourite subjects were math and history. I used to read the Bible, not because it was the Bible but because it had wonderful stories in it.

Q   What is/was your favourite colour?

A   Red, the brightest and most vibrant I could find. It was common for me to have red ribbons in my hair.

Q   What is/was your favourite vegetable?

A   Spinach was my favourite, with tomatoes next.

Q   What were your parents' occupations?

A   Both my parents were shopkeepers and farmers.

Education

I have attained the level of Doctor of Philosophy, specializing in psychology.

Achievements:
• Inter Amicus Human Rights Award, presented by McGill University in Montreal
• The Ryerson University Fellowship
• The Citation of Citizenship
• Honorary Doctor of Laws from the University of Manitoba

1909   African American Matthew Henson is the first polar explorer to discover the North Pole.

73

Daurene Lewis

Daurene Lewis is the first African woman in North America to be elected mayor. She is also an internationally recognized weaver. She is proud of her family connection to another pioneer, Rose Fortune, the first police woman in Canada.

Q   Where were you born?

A   I was born and raised in Annapolis Royal, Nova Scotia.

Q   Who were your role models?

A   My parents were my main role models, but I also used Rose Fortune as someone I should try to be like.

Q   Did you have any hobbies?

A   My main interests were reading and horseback riding. I was very interested in learning about nature and things around me.

Q   What did you wish to be when you were growing up? Why?

A   It was always a goal to grow up and be a medical doctor. I always thought that medicine was fascinating. Being a surgeon was what I had thought the path I saw for myself.

Q   If you could send a message to African Canadian children, what would it be?

A   I would want African Canadian children not to accept limits. If you have a goal, strive to achieve it. You might have difficulty, and the path may not be easy, but if you really want something badly enough, pursue it. Don't wait for doors to be opened for you, push those doors open.

Q   Has racism ever touched you and how did you deal with it?

A   I grew up in the era when discrimination and segregation were all around us. It was very subtle, however, in my community. There were places where if you were African Canadian you just did not go and things you did not do and you knew this.

   In school also if we were reading I would be the student given the role of playing the Black character or thing. I found this very difficult to deal with.

Q   How large was your family when you were growing up?

A   There are three children in our family, two girls and one boy.

Q   Did you and your siblings get along?

A   Because there is a age gap between all of us, we never were extremely close. We all had our own separate friends and hobbies.

Q   Was the push to succeed strong in all the family?

A   The will or desire to succeed was very strong. All the kids knew there were expectations. My mother and her siblings were school teachers, so the view of education and its value as the key to success in the world were around us always.

Q   What did you learn about Black history when you were growing up?

A   Because of my family background, which dates back seven generations, we were fortunate to have a strong oral history tradition. That, along with the fact our early family residence and land holdings are still intact and stories told by my grandparents gave me a great deal of information of life in the Annapolis Royal area.

    The family connection with Rose Fortune being the first police woman was a point of pride that did not go unnoticed.

Q   Did you ever feel separate and different from the other students because of your colour and heritage?

A   Yes I did, mainly because in the community everyone was interested in family history wherever traceable. Because I was only one really to have a genealogy ready-made—I felt our family's contribution to history was there for everyone to see. The knowledge that it was an African Canadian family made it that much better.

Q   What was your favourite subject in school?

A   Math and science.

Q   What is/was your favourite colour?

A   Navy blue has always been a favourite of mine.

Q   What is/was your favourite vegetable?

A   Beets.

Q   What were your parents' occupations?

A   My mother was a teacher and my father was a businessman. He ran a trucking company which started with Rose Fortune. It was the oldest established trucking firm in North America.

Education:

After high school I went on to get my training as a Registered Nurse. I later received a diploma from Dalhousie University allowing me to teach nursing.

Achievements:

• 1979—First African Canadian woman elected to municipal politics
• Doctor of Humane Letters from Mount Saint Vincent University
• Member of the Black Cultural Centre of Nova Scotia's Wall of Honour
• Internationally recognized for weaving
• Administrator in the Homecare Program in the Nova Scotia Department of Health
• 1984—First African woman in North America to be elected mayor

1948   Ruth Bailey and Gwennyth Barton are the first African Canadians to graduate from a Canadian School of Nursing.

75

Joan Jones

This community leader has fought for many years for the equal and fair treatment of African Canadians. She has been a businesswoman and is currently a journalist. Her tireless efforts for causes ranging from civil rights to the better education of all children continue to be an inspiration.

Q   Where were you born?

A   I was born in Boston, Massachusetts, USA. Because of family connections I spent time growing up in Fort Erie, Oakville, and St. Catharines, Ontario, along with Boston and New York City in the USA.

Q   Who were your role models?

A   My parents and my family in both Canada and the U.S. My grandmothers were very important also.

Q   What did you want to be growing up?

A   I always wanted to be a mother like my own who was a stay-at-home mom. No pressure was placed on me to decide a future career. I thought life was always going to be fun.

Q   Did you have any hobbies?

A   I was always very athletic and took part in as many sports as possible.

Q   If you could send a message to African Canadian children, what would it be?

A   I would want our children to be more sure of themselves in the sense of standing up for their rights as people and more vocal in their feeling of self-pride. Our kids have to learn to be responsible for their actions and that there are consequences to the decisions they make.

Q   Has racism ever touched you and how did you deal with it?

A   Racism has been a constant fight throughout my life. It is something all African Canadians deal with. At an early age I began to look for things written by African writers in North America, to learn more about who I was.
It was important to me to also have an opportunity to see famous African American entertainers, to let me see that hard work does have rewards.

Q   How large was your family when you were growing up?

A   There were two children, I have a sister.

Q   Was the push to succeed strong in all the family?

A   My parents passed on to us a strong belief that hard work will lead to success.

Q   What did you learn about Black History when you were growing up?

A   I knew very little about our history, there was none taught in schools. Our family having African American magazines in the house provided most of my education.

Q   Did you ever feel separate and different from the other students because of your race?

A   I always knew I was a different colour. Most (almost all) of the families in the community were white so there were reminders all around us. Being the only African Canadian girl in the community, I needed to be strong and confident in my ability. My parents taught us to take pride in our appearance and wanted us to strive to be the best you could possibly be.

Q   What was your favourite subject in school?

A   I always enjoyed art because it allowed me an opportunity to be creative and make things.

Q   What is your favourite colour?

A   Red.

Q   What was your favourite vegetable as a child?

A   I always enjoyed things like squash and spinach.

Q   What were your parents' occupations?

A   My father worked for a railroad company and my mother was a homemaker.

Achievements
• 1993 Governor General's Award, only the second African Canadian woman to receive this honour. (The first was Dr. Marie Hamilton also from the province of Nova Scotia.)
• Member of the board of Directors of the Izaak Walton Killam Children's Hospital in Halifax

1954   Nova Scotia's Separate School Act is abolished,. African Canadian children and white children can now be taught in the same class.

77

Oliver Jones

Oliver Jones is an internationally acclaimed jazz pianist. He has performed all over the world and is recognized as one of the best for his style, talent, and ability as a performer.

Q   Where were you born?

A   I was born in Montreal, Quebec, and grew up in St. Henry area of the city.

Q   Who were your role models?

A   One person that from an early age, and even through today, serves as a role model is Mr. Oscar Peterson. We both come from similiar background, we even came from the same community. I noticed early on that people embraced the music he played because of his ability and his being a total professional. He symbolizes what can be done with a lot of effort and determination.

   Another person I really looked up to was Jackie Robinson (baseball player). There was one occasion I remember when my father took me to see him play in 1947 when I was 13 years old. The look of pride that my father had when watching him play was one that I will never forget. It didn't really sink in to me the importance of what I was seeing.

Q   Did you have any hobbies?

A   Sports were always a hobby of mine, I especially enjoyed track and field events. Music was something that was always there. I began playing piano at age two and had my first concert at age five.

Q   What did you wish to be when you were growing up? Why?

A   I wanted to be a musician. At that time, however, there were not many opportunities to earn a living at it, so I looked to just get a job.

Q   If you could send a message to African Canadian children what would it be?

A   They are just as important as everyone else, regardless of colour. There are opprtunities out there, but the greatest opportunity that you have is to stay in school. The country is so big there is always going to be a place in it for them. I also want our kids not to use colour as a crutch anymore. If you have qualifications, there is nowhere you can't go or anything you can't do.

Q Has racism ever touched you, and how did you deal with it?

A We all had problems with racism. My father told me from an early age not to let it interfere with what I was doing.

Q How large was your family when you were growing up?

A There were five children originally, but my older brother died when I was quite young. That left my three sisters and me.

Q Did you and your siblings get along?

A We got along like most kids do—sometimes good, sometimes bad. I was a little more spoiled than the girls were.

Q Was the push to succeed strong in all the family?

A My parents always said education was the most important thing in our lives. All the kids seemed to have different talents, and each has been a success in their own right.

Q What did you learn about Black history when you were growing up?

A Nothing at all. It was only after I started to travel that I had an opportunity to explore and learn. My first trip to Nova Scotia at age nine was a shock to me as I didn't think there were any Black people in the rest of the country outside of Montreal. Yet here was a community like Africville and I knew nothing about it.

Q Did you ever feel separate and different from the other students because of your colour and heritage?

A Not in elementary shool, because there was such a large number of Black kids going to the school. In high school I tried not to let the colour issue interfere in friendships I made.

Q What was your favourite subject in school?

A Art, drafting, and music.

Q What is/was your favourite colour?

A Blue.

Q What is/was your favourite vegetable?

A Green peas or corn.

Q What were your parents' occupations?

A My mother came to Canada to work as a housekeeper, and my father worked as a mechanic and welder for the Canadian Pacific Railway.

Achievements
• Member of the Order of Canada, 1994
• Recipient of the Order of Quebec
• Doctorates in Music from Laurentian University in Sudbury, Ont., and McGill University in Montreal
• Recipient of the Oscar Peterson Award, 1989
• Presenter of the first Oscar Peterson Award to Oscar Peterson

1963 Leonard Braithwaite of Ontario becomes the first African Canadian to be elected to a provincial legislature.

79

Almeta Speaks

This accomplished and talented singer and filmmaker has been recognized by many as a leader among African Canadians in the entertainment industry in Canada.

Q   Where were you born?

A   I was born in Reidsville, North Carolina.

Q   Who were your role models?

A   Two teachers in particular: Mrs. Duncan who taught social studies and Mrs. Rogers who taught English. My mother was also a strong role model, along with the women of the church she attended.

Q   Did you have any hobbies?

A   My hobbies included piano, conducting a community choir, and writing stories.

Q   What did you wish to be when you were growing up? Why?

A   My aunt used to buy Black newspapers from Baltimore, Pittsburgh, and New York, and reading them made me want to travel to those cities and some of the European capitals in the articles. Those articles always featured Black people like Bricktop, who owned a nightclub in Rome; Josephine Baker, who performed in Paris, France; and authors like Langston Hughes and Countee Cullens.

Q   If you could send a message to African Canadian children, what would it be?

A   Take time away from the television set to dream. Daydreaming is good. Quiet time in secret places lets you get in touch with yourself. Fantasizing and role playing are excellent games in which to participate. Considering and speculating on your aims and goals are genuine activities that entertain and help create the dreams.

Q   Has racism ever touched you and how did you deal with it?

A   I grew up in a segregated community. Much of our existence was clearly defined. You knew there were certain things you didn't do or places you didn't go. There were times when you were told not to aspire to do things because of the difficulties that may have been caused. This caused many people to be pushed away from their own goals.

   One memory I have is being taught and told by my parents to always use the bathroom before going out. This way I would not have to use the segregated washrooms.

Q   How large was your family when you were growing up?

A   There were eight children, four boys and four girls.

Q   Did you and your siblings get along?

A   We were all encouraged to get along. The closeness of the ages and the fact that our home served as a central location for the rest of the neighbourhood kids to spend time at meant that there was always someone around.

Q   What did you learn about Black history when you were growing up?

A   I was very fortunate that my teachers were very conscious about Black history and willing to teach it. With the school made up the way it was, this sharing of history was very important.

Q   What was your favourite subject in school?

A   History.

Q   What is/was your favourite colour?

A   Black and gold.

Q   What is/was your favourite vegetable?

A   Turnip greens.

Q   What were your parents' occupations?

A   My father worked for the American Tobacco Company factory. My mother ran a day care.

Education

After graduating from high school, I attended University of California at San Diego and received Bachelors Degrees in both Sociology and Communications. I am currently working on my Masters.

Achievements

Two Emmys for TV productions.
Women of Distinction Award in San Diego.

1965   In Essex County, Ont. the last segregated school closes its doors.

81

Jackie Richardson

An accomplished singer and actor, she has worked for many years in a difficult profession where only those who are truly talented can survive. Never one to give up, she has become a role model for her community and for her fans.

Q   Where were you born?

A   I was born in Denora, Pennsylvania, just outside Pittsburgh.

Q   Who were your role models?

A   My mother and grandmother were the two role models I admired the most.

Q   Did you have any hobbies?

A   I loved to read and sing. We sang in the church choir. I began singing professionally at the age of 15.

Q   What did you wish to be when you were growing up? Why?

A   I wanted to be a missionary .My grandparents were devout Baptist people and very involved in the church. They had a lot of influence on me and I thought that kind of work would be rewarding.

Q   If you could send a message to African Canadian children what would it be?

A   Be proud of who you are. Listen to that inner voice to determine if something is right for you. Whatever your goals don't give up, it may be hard if others have their own ideas of what you should do, but you have to be true to yourself. Look to your hobbies for an idea of possible directions you should go as you get older.

Q   Has racism ever touched you, and how did you deal with it?

A   Yes it has. We were the only Black family for approximately 19 years in Richmond Hill, and with that came the battles with people calling us names. We were forced to defend each other as a means of trying to gain the respect of those who would try to put us down.

Q   How large was your family when you were growing up?

A   There were seven children in the family.

Q   Did you and your siblings get along?

A   Around the house we had all the problems kids have with each other, but outside we were very close.

Q   Was the push to succeed strong in all the family?

A   I think the push to succeed was stronger in the girls. The boys seemed to adjust to the community and become more comfortable than we did.

Q   What did you learn about Black history when you were growing up?

A   Very little. I can remember nothing being taught to me. I remember hating learning the history and geography that was taught.

Q   Did you ever feel separate and different from the other students because of your colour and heritage?

A   I was kind of a loner during my school years. So yes, I did feel different.

Q   What was your favourite subject in school?

A   Literature and math.

Q   What is/was your favourite colour?

A   Black, white, and brown.

Q   What is/was your favourite vegetable?

A   Brussels sprouts.

Q   What were your parents' occupations?

A   My father owned his own advertising company; my mother was a homemaker.

Achievements

My greatest achievement is just being an actor/singer. I was very shy as a child and the hardest thing in the world for me was just to get out on a stage.

1974   Dr. Monestine Saint Firmin, of Mattawa, Ontario, becomes the first African Canadian to be elected mayor of a town.

83

Activity

a) After reading all the biographies can you find any similarities among the various role models?

_____

_____

_____

_____

_____

b) Choose one of the role models you admire and give your reasons why you think you are like that person.

_____

_____

_____

_____

_____

_____

_____

_____

I Can Make a Difference

I can make a difference.
Yes, Oh yes, I can;
And my difference, to you,
Could be a promised land.

I can make a difference
To change your point of view.
I can make a difference
And reveal a whole new you.

I can make a difference
In the world of tomorrow.
Yes, I can make that difference
Relieve someone of pain and sorrow.

I can make a difference
In the upcoming world today,
I can make a difference,
But I tell you I must say

That I can make a difference
For the whole world to see,
But to want to make that difference
Has to depend on me.

Tineka Simmons

Activity

Write a poem about your community and the people who live in it.

_____

_____

_____

_____

_____

_____

_____

_____

_____

_____

_____

_____

_____

1978   Stanley Grizzle becomes the first African Canadian to be appointed Citizenship Court Judge in Canada.

Activity

Throughout history, people of African descent all over the world have made their presence felt.

With help from your parents or teachers, and using other books, encyclopedias, and reference material, answer the following questions. Choosing a partner may be helpful.

1. The City of Chicago was founded by this individual.

    _____

2. This person was the first to reach the North Pole.

    _____

3. She was the first African American woman to go into space.

    _____

4. Name four African countries beginning with the letter M.

    _____

    _____

    _____

    _____

5. Africans can be found in the Caribbean. Can you name three countries in this area?

    _____

    _____

    _____

6. In what country are the Great Pyramids found?

    _____

7. What was the real name of Malcolm X?

    _____

8. What country did the Maroons come from?

_____

9. What important landmark in Halifax, Nova Scotia, did they help construct?

_____

10. What do the letters UNIA stand for and who started the organization?

_____

_____

_____

11. What is the name of the first African Canadian to graduate from the Dalhousie University Law School?

_____

12. Born in Russia, this African poet is considered one of the world's greatest writers.

_____

13. He wrote many famous books, including *The Three Musketeers*.

_____

14. He won the first all-race election in South Africa.

_____

15. He was the first African Canadian named Chief Justice in Canada.

_____

16. He led the most famous slave revolt in United States history.

_____

17. This is the largest cultural festival in Canada.

_____

1984   J. Calbert Best becomes High Commissioner for Trinidad and Tobago, the first African Canadian to be appointed as an ambassador.

87

18. This female slave, trying to escape, set fire to the home of her captors. The fire spread to cover half of Montreal. What was her name?

_____

19. He was the first African Canadian to become a lawyer.

_____

20. Name two newspapers dedicated to helping former slaves in Canada.

_____

_____

21. Which province was the first to have a Human Rights Commission?

_____

22. Who was its first director?

_____

23. In 1952, Val Parker was the first African Canadian woman to go to the Olympics. In what city were these Olympics games held?

_____

24. In what city was African American civil rights leader Martin Luther king assassinated?

_____

25. The American Civil Rights movement is said to have started from her actions. Who is this person?

_____

26. This document officially set free the slaves held captive in the United States.

_____

27. This famous American president signed the document referred to in Question 26.

_____

28. The city of Victoria, B.C., used this group as their defence force.

_____

29. This husband and wife led a group of approximately 600 Africans from California to British Columbia in 1858.

_____

_____

30. What is the connection between the colours within the book and the person mentioned in the dedication on page iv ?

_____

1992   Michelle Rawlins becomes the first African Canadian woman to be made a judge of the Ontario Court.

89

Further Reading List

Africville Genealogical Society: *The Spirit of Africville.* Halifax:
A Maritext Book, Formac Publishing Ltd. 1992.

Barton, William F. *Old Plantation Hymns.* Boston, 1899.

Bertley, Leo. *Canada and Its People of African Descent.* Pierrefonds,
Quebec: Bilongo Publishers, 1977.

Ffrench, Robert. *Out of The Past, Into the Future.*
Dartmouth: Pride Communications, 1994.

Hill, Lawrence. *Trials and Triumphs: The story of African Canadians.*
Toronto: Umbrella Press, 1993.

Hudson, Wade and Wesley, Valerie W. *Afro Bets: Book of Black Heroes from A to Z.*
New Jersey: Just Us Books, 1988.

Johnson, James Weldon and Johnson, J. Rosamond. *The Book of American
Negro Spirituals and the Second Book of Negro Spirituals.* New York, 1925, 1926.
Issued in one volume, New York: 1969.

Ringgold, Faith. *Aunt Harriet's Underground Railroad in the Sky.*
New York: Crown Publishers Inc., 1992.

Sadlier, Rosemary. *Leading the Way: Black Women in Canada.*
Toronto: Umbrella Press, 1994.

Southern, Eileen. *The Music of Black America.* New York: 1971.

Further Resources

There are many groups and organizations whose goal is to further African Canadian culture and history. Here are some some examples.

The Cultural Awareness Youth Group (Nova Scotia)

The Cultural Awareness Youth Group was founded in 1983 and is an independent, non-profit society dedicated to the cultural, educational, and career development of Black youth in Nova Scotia.

With chapters in various Halifax and area schools the goals of the CAYG are

- to promote the learning of Black history and culture among Black youth and the general community
- to provide activities of interest to Black youth
- to provide avenues through which Black youth can deal with problems of identity
- to promote a strong positive identify for Black youth
- to promote cultural sharing and exchange between Black youth and the general community
- to promote educational and career development for Black youth

While it is advised by a volunteer Adult Community Board, the direction the various groups take is determined by the students involved. The CAYG has presented community workshops, films, cultural shows, and more in its efforts to make a difference.

The CAYG had its efforts recognized in 1986 when it received the Commonwealth Award for Youth Development.

For further information, contact:

Cultural Awareness Youth Group
2099 Gottingen Street
Suite 205
Halifax, N.S.   B3K 3B2

(902) 425-0287

1993   Wayne Adams become the first African Canadian elected to the Nova Scotia Provincial Legislature.

The Black Educators Association of Manitoba (BEAM)

The Black Educators Association of Manitoba consists of educators devoted to the promotion of quality education and the development of equal opportunities for students.

The organization is committed to the educational advancement of African Canadians by

- providing a forum for the exchange of ideas
- assisting in the development of materials that reflect the multicultural nature of society
- assisting the proper assessment and placement of students new to the school system
- acting as spokespersons for educators and students
- monitoring the educational curriculum and materials used to ensure that students are portrayed with dignity and fairness.

For further information, contact

Black Educators Association of Manitoba
P.O. Box 1131
Winnipeg, Man. R3C 2Y4

Canadian Artists Network: Black Artists in Action (CANBAIA)

The Canadian Artists Network was founded in Toronto in the fall of 1988. Born of the belief that the richness and diversity of Black art is an essential element of Canadian culture, the Canadian Artists Network (Black Artists in Action) was formed with the purpose of promoting the works and efforts of the Black artist in Canada. Like their counterparts throughout the world, Blacks in Canada have discovered that producing their work is far too often only the first step in an exceedingly difficult struggle to find acceptance for their art. Despite the obstacles Black art continues to flourish. It is this in spirit of determined dignity and the need for positive images for Black youth, both in Canada and abroad, that CANBAIA was formed.

For further information, contact

Canadian Artists Network: Black Artists in Action
183 Bathurst St.
Toronto, Ont.   M5T 2R7

(416) 369-9040

Glossary

Abolitionist — A person who opposed slavery and worked to end it.

Akee — Tropical fruit eaten as a cooked vegetable that looks and tastes like scrambled eggs

American Civil War — War fought between the northern US states (the Union) and the Confederate States of the South, 1861–65. Slavery, which was allowed in the South, was one of the causes of the war.

Ancestor — A member of the same family who lived very long ago.

Bantu — A group of people living in central and southern Africa.

Breadfruit — Starchy tropical fruit that tastes like bread when baked.

Catalyst — Person or thing that causes a change to occur.

Community — A group of individuals living in a particular place and sharing common interests.

Dietician — Person trained to plan healthy meals.

Discrimination — Treating someone differently or unfairly because of differences such as race, colour, or gender.

Economics — The science of how wealth (things that have a money value) is produced and shared out.

Genealogy — The study of a family from an ancestor to the present generation; a family tree.

Generation — A stage in the history of a family; all the people born at about the same time.

Hausa — A group of African people living in the Sudan and northern Nigeria.

Heritage — Something handed down by one's ancestors.

Homestead — Area of land granted to a settler under certain conditions.

Hostage — A person held captive against their will.

Human Rights Commission — A group set up by a government to ensure that people are treated fairly.

Integrate — To make facilities (such as a school) available to all people; the opposite of segregate.

King's Counsel — Title given to a lawyer to reward good service (also Queen's Counsel).

Maroons — Escaped slaves in the Caribbean who lived together and fought to avoid recapture. A group of Maroons from Jamaica came to Canada in 1796. (See *Out of the Past Into the Future*.)

Masai — A group of people living in the area of Africa that is now Kenya and Tanzania.

Mi'kmaq — A group of Native people living in Atlantic Canada.

Missionary — A person sent by a church to another country or area to teach the religion to others.

Nubian — A group of African people living in southern Egypt and northern Sudan.

Orator — A person who speaks very well in public.

Pickanninny — A racist and insulting term for an African child.

Plaintain — A tropical fruit related to the banana that is cooked and eaten as a vegetable.

Racism — The unfounded belief that one race of people is better than another.

Revolt — A fight by a people against their leader or government.

Revolutionary War — Also called the American War of Independence, or American Revolution, the revolt of American colonies against British rule, 1775–83, which ended with the United States of America becoming a separate country.

Segregate — To separate or set apart from others; to separate one racial group from the rest of a community.

Sibling — A brother or sister.

Sierra Leone — Country on the coast of West Africa that became home to a number of former slaves. Its capital is Freetown.

Slave trade — The buying and selling of human beings for profit.

Slave — A human being whose freedom has been stolen and who is owned by another.

Speaker — Member of a legislature or parliament who is chosen to be in charge of debate and other business.

Suffrage — The right to vote.

Terminal — The last stop on a railway line.

Underground Railroad — Secret system set up by abolitionists in Canada and the United States to help slaves escape to freedom. (See *Out of the Past Into the Future*.)

United Empire Loyalists — People who did not want to remain in the United States when that country separated from Britain. Many settled in New Brunswick, Nova Scotia, and Ontario.

Upper Canada — Part of Canada that became Ontario.

Uprising — A revolt (see above).

Yam — Starchy root vegetable eaten in the tropics.

Zulu — A group of people living in South Africa in the area that is now north-eastern Natal.

1994 *Out of the Past, Into the Future* is published. It is the first book on African Canadian history designed for the elementary school age reader in Canada.

93

Answers

Break the Code, p. 8
1. Frederick Douglass
2. Alice Walker
3. Martin Luther King
4. Hausa [Legend]
5. Harriet Tubman
6. Aesop
7. Billie Holiday
8. Marcus Garvey
9. Malcolm X

Quiz, p. 88
1. Jean Baptiste Dusable
2. Matthew Henson
3. Mae Jemison
4. Mozambique, Mali, Mauritania, Morocco
5. Cuba, Trinidad, Haiti, Jamaica, Antigua, Barbados, etc.
6. Egypt
7. Malcolm Little
8. Jamaica
9. Maroon Bastion, Citadel Hill

10. United Negro Improvement Association (started by Marcus Garvey)
11. James Robinson Johnson
12. Alexander Pushkin
13. Alexandre Dumas
14. Nelson Mandela
15. Julius Alexander Isaac
16. Nat Turner
17. Caribana
18. Marie Joseph Angelique
19. Delos Rogest Davis
20. *Provincial Freeman*; *Voice of the Fugitive*
21. Ontario
22. Daniel Hill
23. Helsinki
24. Memphis, Tennessee, April 4, 1968
25. Rosa Parks
26. Emancipation Proclamation
27. Abraham Lincoln
28. Victoria Pioneer Rifle Company
29. Louis and Sylvia Stark
30. Civil rights leader Marcus Garvey was born in Jamaica. That country's flag is green, yellow, and black.